Avgusta Udar

EASY PIANO SHEET MUSIC FOR KIDS
+ Mini-course
"How to Play Keyboard"

FREE AUDIO

+BONUS 15 SONGS

Beginner Piano Songbook
for Children and Teens with 60 Songs.
First Book Step by Step

See all of our books, promotions, and new releases at:

amazon.com/author/avgusta

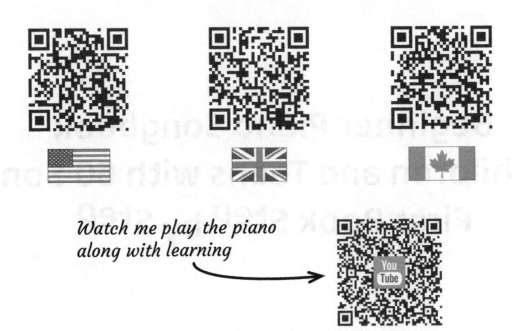

Watch me play the piano along with learning

Messages about typos, errors, inaccuracies and suggestions for improving the quality are gratefully received at:
avgustaudartseva@gmail.com

CONTENTS

Introduction 7

Chapter 1

Mini-course "How to Play Keyboard" 9

1. The Stave (Staff), Notes and Treble Clef 11
2. Ledger Lines and Octave 14
3. Notes on the Keyboard (layout) 15
4. Note Values 16
5. ⁴₄ Time Signature. Measure, Bar Line 21
6. Rests Whole, Half, Quarter, Eighth 23
7. ²₄ Time Signature 26
8. ³₄ Time Signature 28
9. Numbering of Measures 29
10. Incomplete Measure 31
11. Dotted Note 35
12. ⁶₈ Time Signature 36
13. Ties and Slurs 38

Chapter 2

A Collection of Songs. Practice 41

1. Alphabet Song 43
2. God Is So Good 44
3. O When The Saints 45
4. Sleep, Baby Sleep 46
5. Lovely Evening 47
6. A-Tisket, A-Tasket 48

7. Twinkle Twinkle Little Star 49

8. Humpty Dumpty 50

9. Hickory Dickory Dock 51

10. London Bridge Is Falling Down 52

11. Baa, Baa, Black Sheep 53

12. Skip To My Lou 54

13. Mary Had A Little Lamb 55

14. Muffin Man 56

15. Jennie Jenkins 57

16. Ten Little Indians 58

17. Billy Boy 59

18. The Farmer In The Dell 60

19. Do Your Ears Hang Low? 61

20. Pop! Goes the Weasel 62

21. The Wheels On The Bus 63

22. Happy Birthday 64

23. This Old Man 65

24. Rain, Rain, Go Away 66

25. Old MacDonald Had A Farm 67

26. Jingle Bells 68

27. We Wish You A Merry Christmas 69

28. Simple Gifts 70

29. Oh, Dear! What Can The Matter Be? 71

30. O Christmas Tree 72

31. Hush Little Baby 73

32. Away In A Manger 74

33. Bingo 75

34. She'll Be Coming Round The Mountain 76

35. Vacation Days 77

36. America 78

37. Buffalo Gals 79

38. Silent Night 80

39. The North Wind Doth Blow 81

40. Rock-a-Bye Baby 82

41. Keemo Kymo 83

42. The Teddy Bears' Picnic 84

43. I've Got Peace Like A River 85

44. Head, Shoulders, Knees and Toes 86

45. Shenandoah 87

46. Clementine 88

47. Long, Long Ago 89

48. If You're Happy And You Know It 90

49. All The Pretty Little Horses 91

50. My Bonnie Lies Over The Ocean 92

51. Jolly Old Saint Nicholas 93

52. Yankee Doodle 94

53. Cindy 95

54. Old Dan Tucker 96

55. The Cuckoo 97

56. Aura Lee 98

57. Golden Sun.. 99

58. All Through The Night........................ 100

59. America The Beautiful........................ 101

60. Come, All Ye Young Sailormen 102

☺ Your Bonus.. 103

Glossary of a Beginner Musician................ 105

EASY PIANO SHEET MUSIC

THIS BOOK BELONGS TO:

_____

_____

_____

Introduction

This collection of easy tunes for keyboard or piano designed for children and older beginners. The initial tunes use only 5-6 different notes but by the end of the book the tunes range to over on octave with some sharps and flats also begin used.

This book contains light songs, you can play them after studying the introductory theoretical material at the beginning of the book. All songs in this book are written in the treble clef. The music theory mini-beginner course focuses exceptionally on the degree of difficulty of the songs in this book.

Dedicated to my children Agatha and Myron

Chapter 1

Mini-course
"How to Play Keyboard"

* Staff and Stave: have the same value. Staff is more common in American English, Stave in British English. For the purposes of this book, we use Stave, don't worry if your country uses Staff, you can just cross out Stave and replace it with Staff.

1. The Stave (Staff), Notes and Treble Clef

Music is written on a set of 5 lines called a STAVE (STAFF).

The TREBLE CLEF

The Stave (Staff)

The two clefs that are basically used are the treble clef and the bass clef. In this book, the melodies of the songs are written only in the treble clef.

Music Notes are oval-shaped symbols that are placed on the lines, or in spaces between them.

They represent musical sounds, called *PITCHES.*

Notes on the line

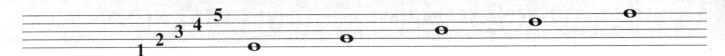

Notes in the spaces

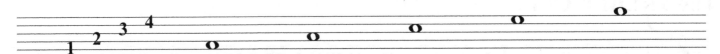

The lines of the stave are numbered from bottom to top (1-5). The spaces between the lines are also numbered from bottom to top (1-4).

If the notes appear higher on the stave, they sound higher in pitch. If the notes appear lower on the stave, they sound lower in pitch.

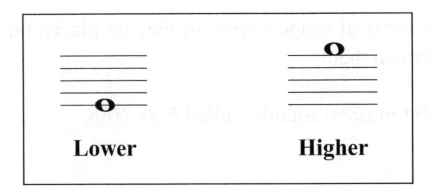

Music notes are named after the first seven letters of the alphabet:
A, B, C, D, E, F, G.

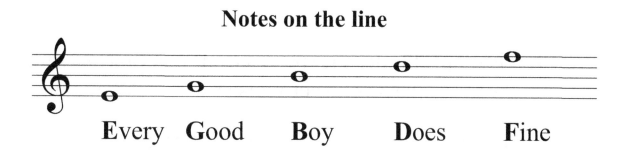

In the treble stave, the names of the notes on the lines from bottom to top are **E, G, B, D, F.**

Notes on the line

Every   Good   Boy   Does   Fine

The names of the notes in the spaces from bottom to top spell **FACE.**

Notes in the spaces

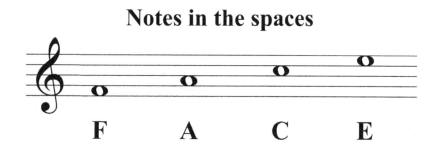

F   A   C   E

* On page 109 and 111 you will find letters **A B C D E F G** that can be printed at home, cut out and temporarily glued to double-sided tape or glue, which can then be easily removed from the keys. There are ready-made kits on sale on Amazon that we recommend you buy. Just search for: *piano keyboard stickers.*

P.S. Choose glue or tape that can be easily removed from the keys afterwards. If in doubt, it is better not to glue it yourself and order ready-made stickers from Amazon.

2. Ledger Lines and Octave

Ledger lines are those little lines with notes on them that appear above or below a musical stave (staff):

The purpose of these lines is to extend the stave in both directions, up and down.

An *OCTAVE* is simply the distance between one note and that same note repeated in the next higher or lower register within the audible range.

The following reference table shows how to find the keyboard notes frequently used in this book:

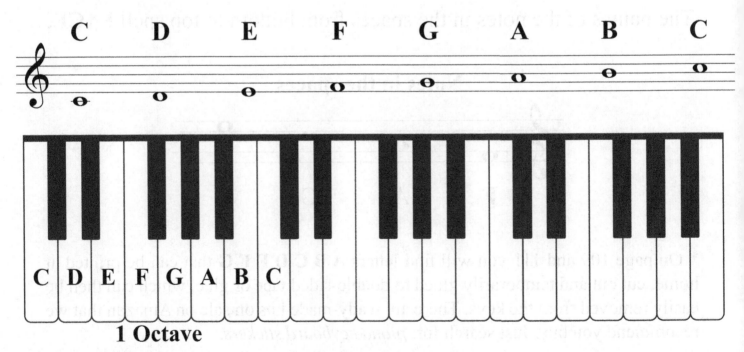

Note registers therefore are groups of the same notes that are repeated across the audible range.

14

In this book, songs are performed not only using white keys, but also there are notes that must be played on the keyboard using black keys (sharp ♯, flat ♭).

The *SHARP* sign (♯) before a note raises the pitch of that note. On the keyboard, play the next black key to the right. If the note F has a ♯ sign, then we play the black key closest to the right.

The *FLAT* sign (♭) before a note lowers the pitch of that note. On the keyboard, play the next black key to the left. If the note E has the sign ♭, then we play the black key closest to the left.

For those who still learning to read music and memorize where a note is on the keyboard, the following reference table shows how to find the notes on the keyboard used in this book.

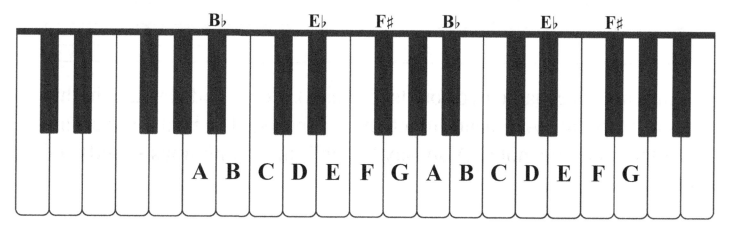

While the placement of notes on the stave indicates the pitch, the duration of the note (how long the note is held down) is determined by the value of the note.

A *WHOLE NOTE* is drawn as an open oval.	**Whole note** 𝗈

A whole note is equal to four counts (or beats). Count and clap the rhythm evenly (hands together for 4 beats). The beat numbers are written under the notes. Also, say "ta-ah-ah-ah" (in a continuous sound) and clap.

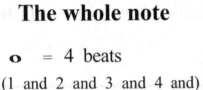

The whole note

𝗈 = 4 beats

(1 and 2 and 3 and 4 and)

The whole note

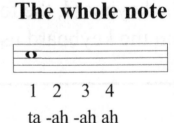

1 2 3 4

ta -ah -ah ah

Two *HALF NOTES* are equal the duration of one whole note.	**Half notes**

A half note is equal to two counts (or beats). Count and clap the rhythm evenly (holding your hands together for 2 beats). The beat numbers are written under the notes. Also, say "ta-ah" (in a continuous sound) and clap.

16

The half note
♩ = 2 beats
(1 and 2 and)

1 2   3 4
ta -ah   ta -ah

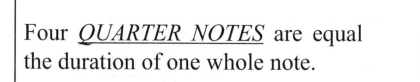

Quarter notes

Four *QUARTER NOTES* are equal the duration of one whole note.

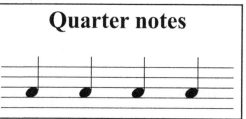

A quarter note is equal to one count (or beat). Count (1, 2, 3, 4) and clap the rhythm evenly (once per beat). The beat numbers are written under the notes. Also, say "ta" and clap.

The quarter note
♩ = 1 beat (1 and)

The quarter notes

1   2   3   4
ta   ta   ta   ta

o   =   ♩ ♩   =   ♩ ♩ ♩ ♩

1 Whole   2 Half Notes   4 Quarter Notes
Note

Stems extend downward on the left side when the note appears on or above the 3rd line of the stave. Stems extend upward on the right side when the note appears below the 3rd line of the stave.

Stems Up   Stems Down

17

When you add a flag to the stem of a quarter note, it becomes an *EIGHTH NOTE*.

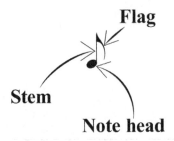

Flag

Stem

Note head

Eighth notes

Two *EIGHTH NOTES* are equal the duration of one quarter note.

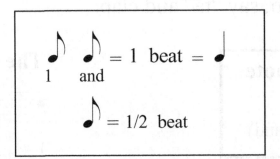

An eighth note is equal to one-half count (or beat).
Count (1 and 2 and 3 and 4 and) and clap the rhythm evenly (once per beat and once per "and"). The beat numbers are written under the notes. Also, say "ti" and clap.

Count: 1   and   2   and   3   and   4   and
             ti   ti   ti   ti   ti   ti   ti   ti

Two eighth notes equal 1 quarter note

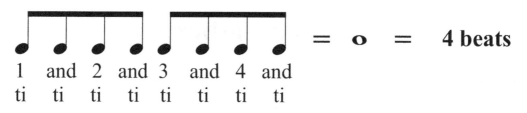

♪ ♪ = ♩ = **1 beat**

1   and
ti   ti

Four eighth notes equal 1 half note

= ♩ = **2 beats**

1   and   2   and
ti   ti   ti   ti

Eight eighth notes equal 1 whole note

= o = **4 beats**

1   and   2   and   3   and   4   and
ti   ti   ti   ti   ti   ti   ti   ti

Two or more 8th notes are connected by a beam.

Beam

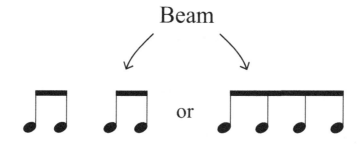

or

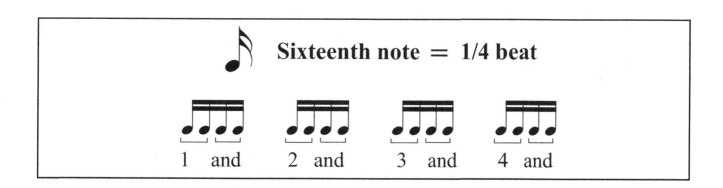

♪ **Sixteenth note = 1/4 beat**

1   and   2   and   3   and   4   and

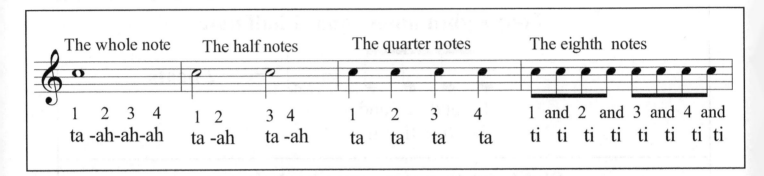

Remember:

Whole note	o = 4 beats (1 and 2 and 3 and 4 and)
Half note	♩ = 2 beats (1 and 2 and)
Quarter note	♩ = 1 beat 1 and
Eighth note	♪ = 1/2 beat ♪ ♪ = 1 beat 1 and
Sixteenth note	♬ = 1/4 beat ♬♬ = 1 beat 1 and

The *TIME SIGNATURE* appears at the beginning of the music after the clef sign. It contains two numbers, one above the other.

The upper number tells how many beats (or counts) are in each measure. In this case, 4.

The lower number indicates what type of note receives 1 beat. In this case, a quarter note.

The two numbers in the time signature are often replaced by the letter **C** .

$$\frac{4}{4} = C$$

So, play the melody (presented in this collection) with your right hand and say the beats signed under the sheet music:

7. Twinkle Twinkle Little Star

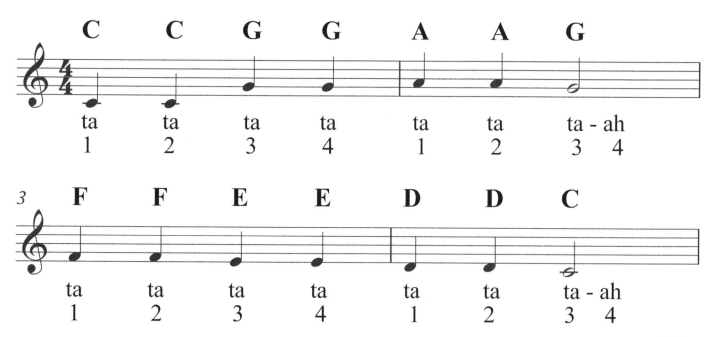

Music is divided into equal parts by *BAR LINES.* The area between the two bar lines is called a *MEASURE* or *BAR.*

Measures   or   bar

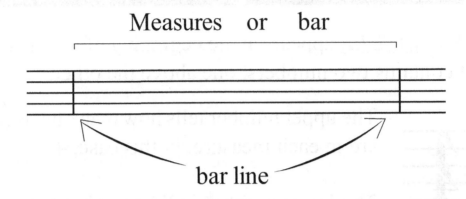

bar line

A *DOUBLE BAR* is written at the end of a piece of music. It is made up of one thin and one thick line, with the thick line always on the outside.

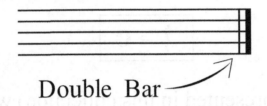

Double Bar

Measures   or   bar

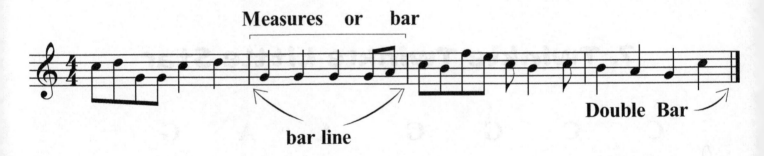

bar line

Double Bar

Music is not only made up of sounds, but also the silence between sounds. The duration of musical silence is determined by the value of the *REST.*

A *WHOLE REST* means to rest for a whole measure. It hangs down from the 4th line.	
A *HALF REST* is equal to half of a whole rest. It sits on the 3rd line.	
A *QUARTER REST* is equal to one quarter of a whole rest.	

In 4/4 Time:

Quarter rests are equal to 1 beat.	1 2 3 4
Half rests are equal to 2 beats.	1 2 3 4
Whole rests are equal to 4 beats.	1 2 3 4

An *EIGHTH REST* 𝄾 is equal to half the value of a quarter rest 𝄽

Two 8th rests equal 1 quarter rest   𝄾   𝄾 = 𝄽
         1   and

Four 8th rests equal 1 half rest   𝄾 𝄾 𝄾 𝄾 =
         1 and 2 and

Eight 8th rests equal 1 whole rest   𝄾 𝄾 𝄾 𝄾 𝄾 𝄾 𝄾 𝄾 =
         1 and 2 and 3 and 4 and

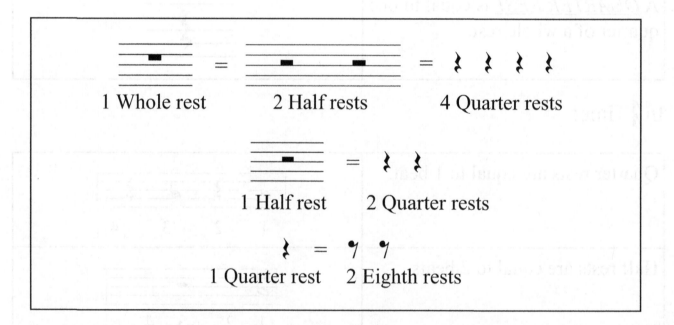

An Sixteenth rest is equal to half the value of a eighth rest

Remember:

Notes		Rests
Whole note	$\mathbf{o}$ = 𝄻	**Whole rest**
Half note	𝅗𝅥 = 𝄼	**Half rest**
Quarter note	𝅘𝅥 = 𝄽	**Quarter rest**
Eighth note	𝅘𝅥𝅮 = 𝄾	**Eighth rest**
Sixteenth note	𝅘𝅥𝅯 = 𝄿	**Sixteenth rest**

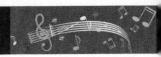

$\frac{2}{4}$ 2 means that there are 2 beats per measure;
4 means that the quarter note receives 1 beat.

$\frac{2}{4}$ and $\frac{4}{4}$ both have 4 as the bottom number, meaning a quarter note receives 1 beat.

<u>The difference is that:</u> $\frac{2}{4}$ has 2 beats per measure while $\frac{4}{4}$ has 4.

Count: 1   2   1   2   1   2   1   2

A whole rest is used for a full measure of rest, even if there are only 2 beats in each measure. When writing the music, a half rest and a whole note are never used in $\frac{2}{4}$ time.

So, play the melody (presented in this collection) with your right hand and say the beats signed under the sheet music:

10. London Bridge Is Falling Down

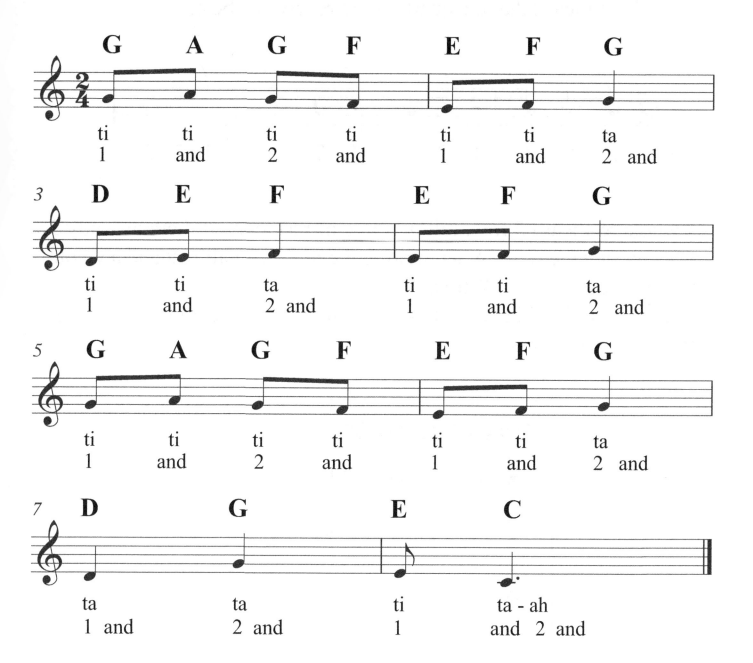

3 3 means that there are 3 beats per measure;
4 4 means that the quarter note receives 1 beat.

Count: 1   2   3   1   2   3   1   2   3   1   2   3

A whole rest is used for a full measure of rest, even if there are only 3 beats in each measure. When writing the music, a half rest and a whole note are never used in ¾ time.

²⁄₄ , ³⁄₄ and ⁴⁄₄ all have 4 as the bottom number, meaning the quarter note always receives 1 beat.

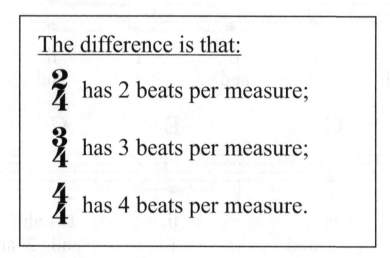

The difference is that:

2⁄4 has 2 beats per measure;

3⁄4 has 3 beats per measure;

4⁄4 has 4 beats per measure.

9. Numbering of Measures

In this collection, the bars in each song are numbered. At the beginning of each next line of notes, a number is placed above the treble clef, which indicates the number of the measure.

1. Alphabet Song

The numbering of measures in the first note line is not indicated.

1. Alphabet Song

10. Incomplete Measure

A *MEASURE* is a unit of music. It is the space (area of music) between two bar lines. The time signature (the 2 numbers at the beginning of the melody) indicates how many beats are in a measure.

A first measure is called an *INCOMPLETE MEASURE* when it does not contain the full number of beats as indicated by the time signature.

The notes in the first Incomplete measure (the part of the counts found at the beginning of the music) are called the anacrusis, pick-up or upbeat.

An incomplete measure is measure that is split or divided between the beginning and the end of the music.

Part of the measure is found at the beginning of the music. The remaining part of the measure is found at the end of the music.

The two "parts" must add up to one complete (full) measure.

$\frac{4}{4}$ = 4 beats per measure.

6. A-Tisket, A-Tasket

First incomplete measure

Last incomplete measure

When a melody starts with an Incomplete measure, it does not start with count #1!

Count #1 is the first count of the first complete measure. It is not necessarily the first count of the melody.

So, how is the first count of an incomplete measure? To figure this out, you must go to the end, to the last measure!

$\frac{3}{4}$ = 3 beats per measure.

22. Happy Birthday

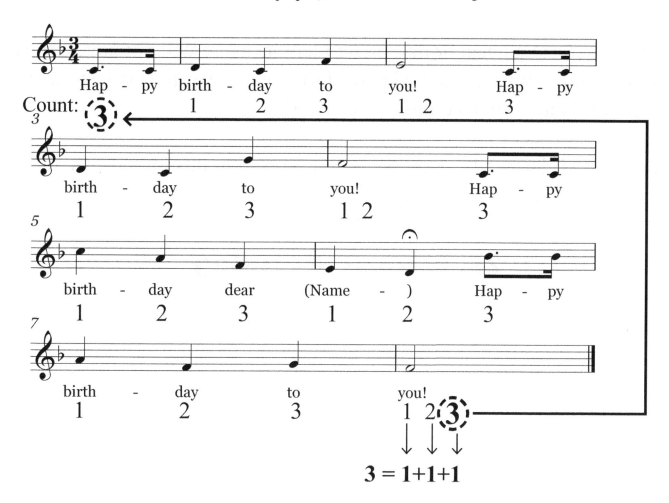

The beginning of the final measure will be count #1. So, start adding the counts there and, when you run out of beats, head back to the beginning and finish adding the counts.

The final measure will start with count #1. Start adding the counts there and, when they run out of notes to write counts under, they get to head back to the beginning to finish the counting.

Why do we use an incomplete measure? Quite simply, it is all about the beat and the pulse. Trying singing "Happy Birthday" but start with a strong downbeat (strong pulse) instead of with a weak upbeat (weak pulse). It just does not sound correct, does it?

The important tip to remember is that measure #1 is the first measure that has count #1! The first measure may not be measure #1. If there is no count #1 at the beginning of that measure, then it is an incomplete measure.

The anacrusis, upbeat or first incomplete measure will not have a measure number. It is considered part of the final measure (the last incomplete measure) when counting measures.

So, while it looks like there are 9 "measures" in this melody, there are only 8 "Complete" measures.

22. Happy Birthday

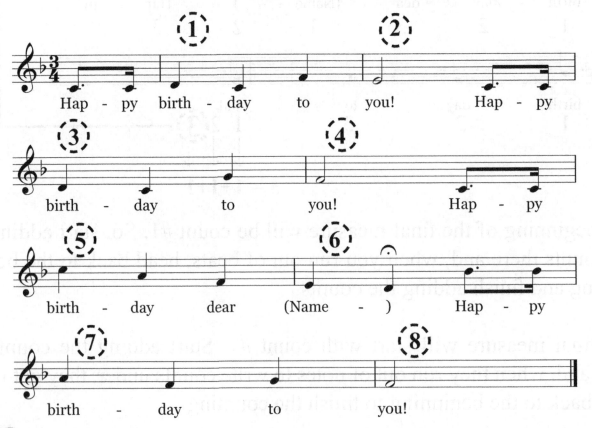

In music, there is a note with a dot, and in our collection, notes with a dot are also found in songs.

A dot that is placed after the note to indicate a change in the duration of a note. The dot adds half of the value of the note to itself. For example, a dotted half note gets 3 beats - value of a half note is 2, half of 2 is 1 so 2 + 1 = 3.

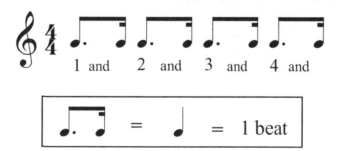

Dotted rhythms mix longer dotted notes with shorter undotted notes.

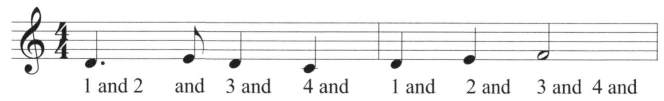

So, play the melody (presented in this collection) with your right hand and say the beats signed under the sheet music:

52. Yankee Doodle

12. $\frac{6}{8}$ Time Signature

$\frac{6}{8}$ 6 means that there are 6 beats per measure;
        8 means that the eight note receives 1 beat.

How to count in $\frac{6}{8}$:

There are two ways to count a bar in $\frac{6}{8}$ time. This can seem too much confusing, when you first encounter $\frac{6}{8}$, but as we'll see the difference is not as big as it first appears.

You can either count it as:

- 6 eighth-note beats: 1, 2, 3, 4, 5, 6 = 1, 2, 3, 1, 2, 3
- 2 dotted-quarter-note beats: 1… 2…

Now you try: Clap and say the beats:

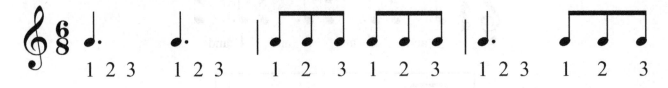

So, play the melody (presented in this collection) with your right hand and say the beats signed under the sheet music:

29. Oh, Dear! What Can The Matter Be?

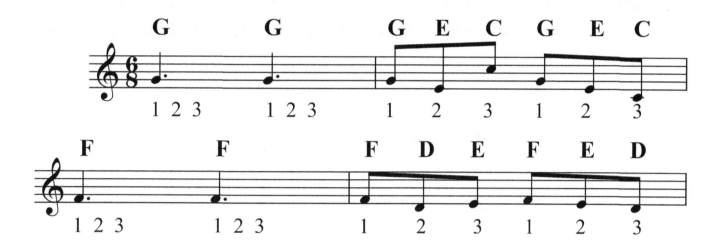

13. Ties and Slurs

A *TIE* joins two notes of the same pitch by a curved line over or under the notes. Each note joined by a tie is held for its full value but only the first note is played or sung. The tied note's value is added to the value of the first note.

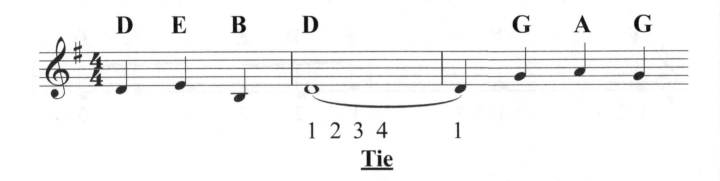

50. My Bonnie Lies Over The Ocean

The tie should always be written on the opposite side from the note stems.

38

A *SLUR* smoothly connects two or more notes of different pitches by a curved line over or under the notes. There is no break in sound between pitches. This is also called playing or singing *LEGATO.*

17. Billy Boy

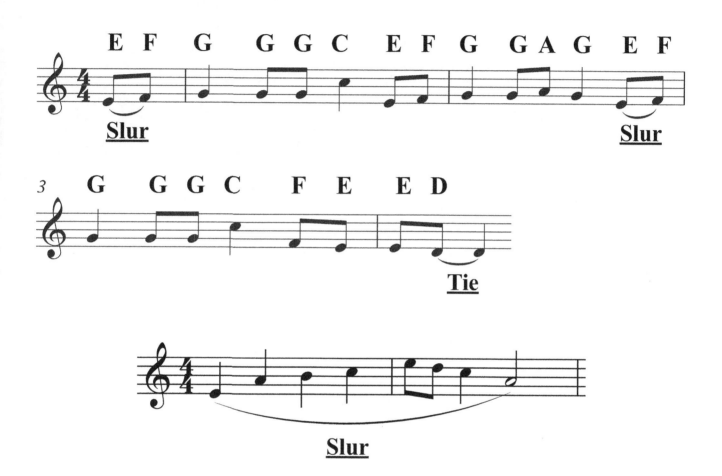

Chapter 2

A Collection of Songs.
Practice*

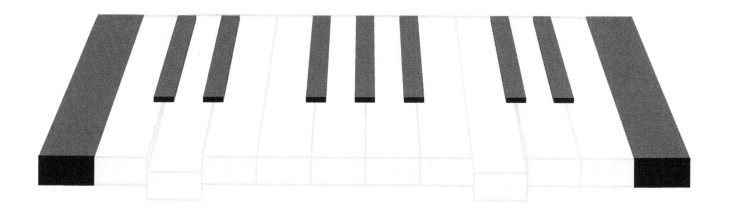

* If it is not convenient for you to play the songs from the book, then go to page 103, there you will find all the songs in PDF format and you can print any of them or open them on a tablet.

1. Alphabet Song

2. God Is So Good

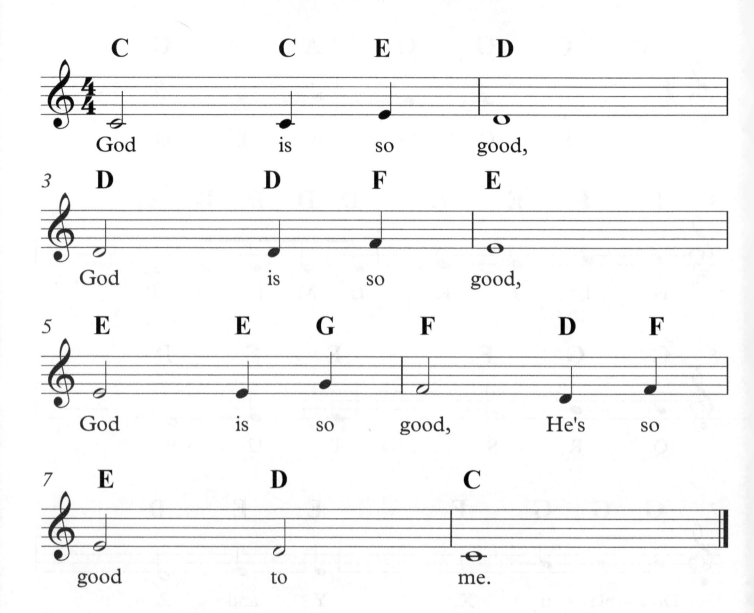

3. O When The Saints

4. Sleep, Baby Sleep

2. Sleep, baby, sleep.
Our cottage vale is deep.
The little lamb is on the green
With snowy fleece so soft and clean
Sleep, baby, sleep.

5. Lovely Evening

6. A-Tisket, A-Tasket

7. Twinkle Twinkle Little Star

49

8. Humpty Dumpty

Hump - ty Dump - ty sat on a wall.

Hump - ty Dump - ty had a great fall.

All the king's hor - ses and all the king's men

could - n't put Hump - ty to - ge - ther a - gain.

50

9. Hickory Dickory Dock

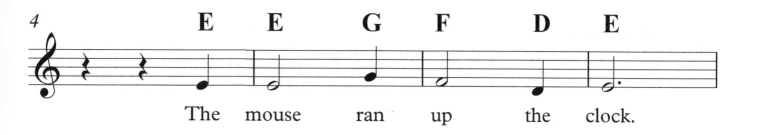

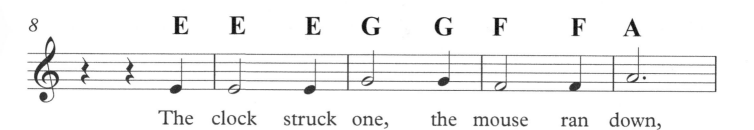

10. London Bridge Is Falling Down

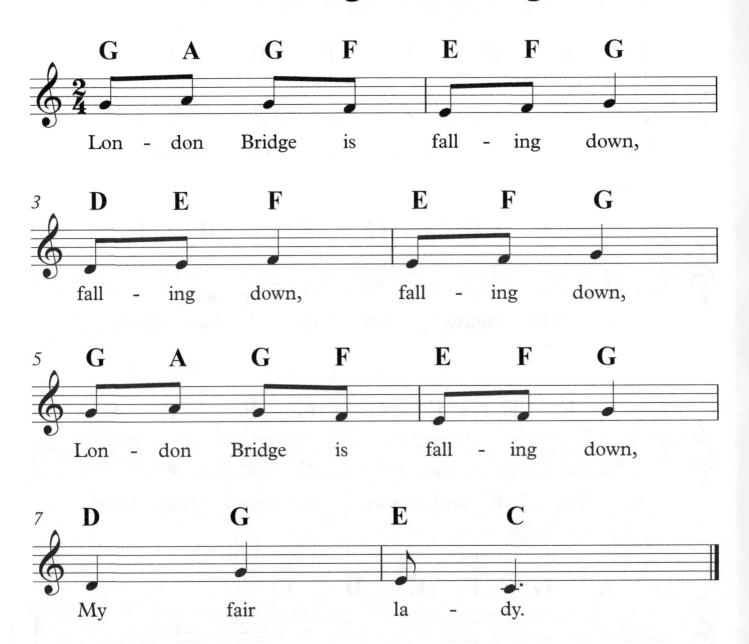

11. Baa, Baa, Black Sheep

53

12. Skip To My Lou

13. Mary Had A Little Lamb

14. Muffin Man

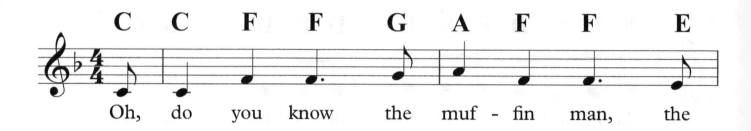

15. Jennie Jenkins

Will you wear white, Oh my dear, Oh my dear?

Will you wear white, Jen - nie Jen - kins? No, I

won't wear white, for the col - ors, too bright,

I'll___ buy me a fol - de - rol - dy, til - de - tol - dy, seek - a - dou - ble,

use - a - cause - a, roll - a - find - me, roll,_____ Jen - nie Jen - kins, roll.

16. Ten Little Indians

2. Ten little, nine little, eight little Indians,
   Seven little, six little, five little Indians,
   Four little, three little, two little Indians,
   One little Indian boy.

17. Billy Boy

18. The Farmer In The Dell

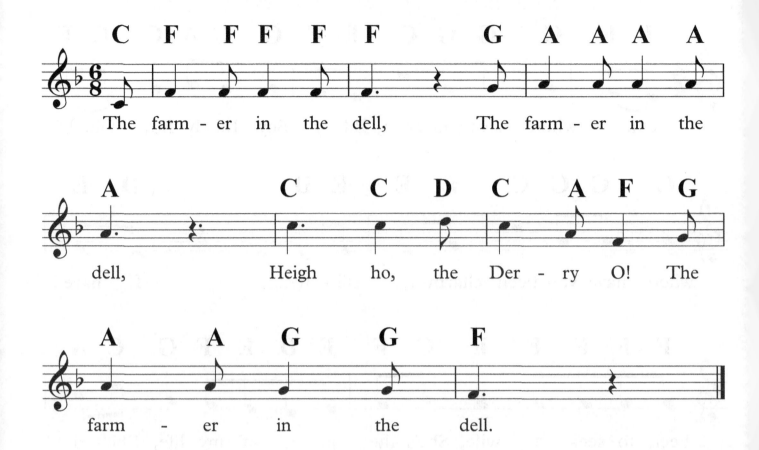

2. The farmer takes the wife
   The farmer takes the wife
   Heigh ho, the Derry O!
   The farmer takes the wife.

19. Do Your Ears Hang Low?

20. Pop! Goes the Weasel

F   F   G   G   A   C   A

All   a - round   the   mul - ber - ry

F   C   F   F   G   G

bush,   the   mon - key   chased   the

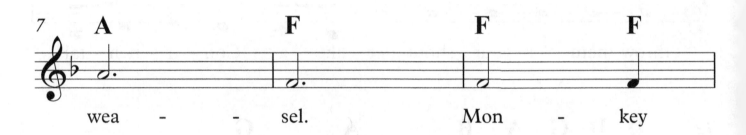

A   F   F   F

wea - - sel.   Mon - key

G   G   A   C   A   F

stopped   to   pull   up   his   sock.

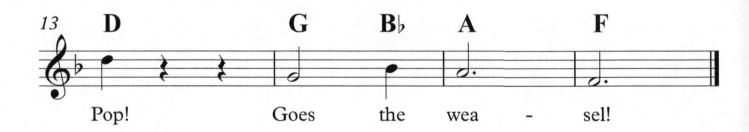

D   G   B♭   A   F

Pop!   Goes   the   wea - sel!

21. The Wheels On The Bus

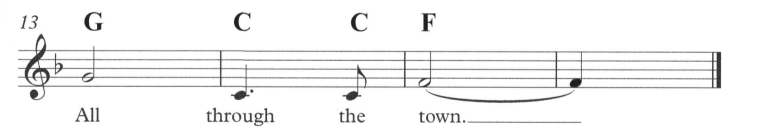

22. Happy Birthday

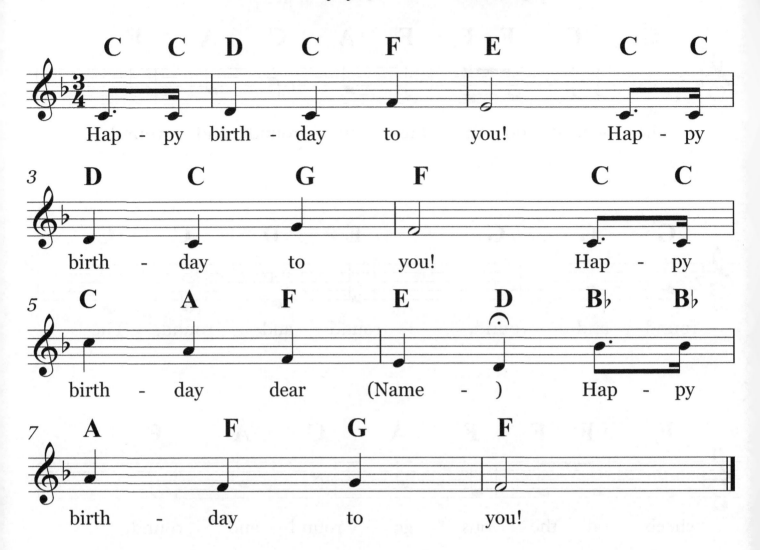

23. This Old Man

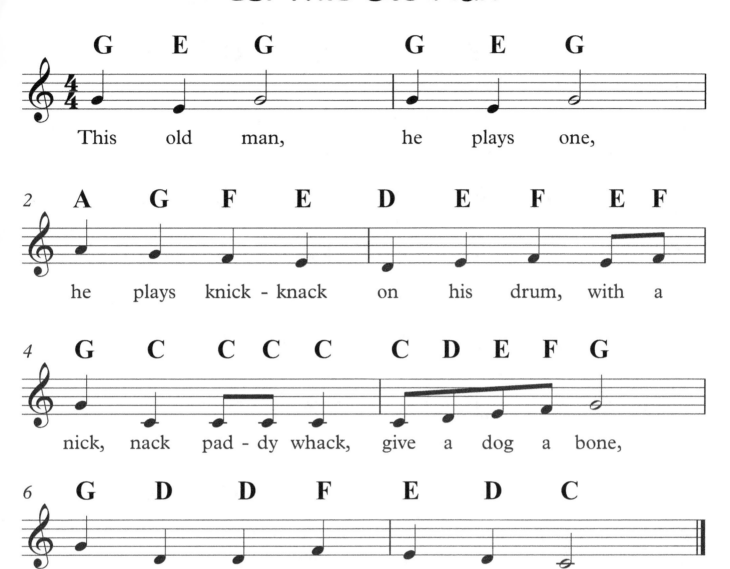

24. Rain, Rain, Go Away

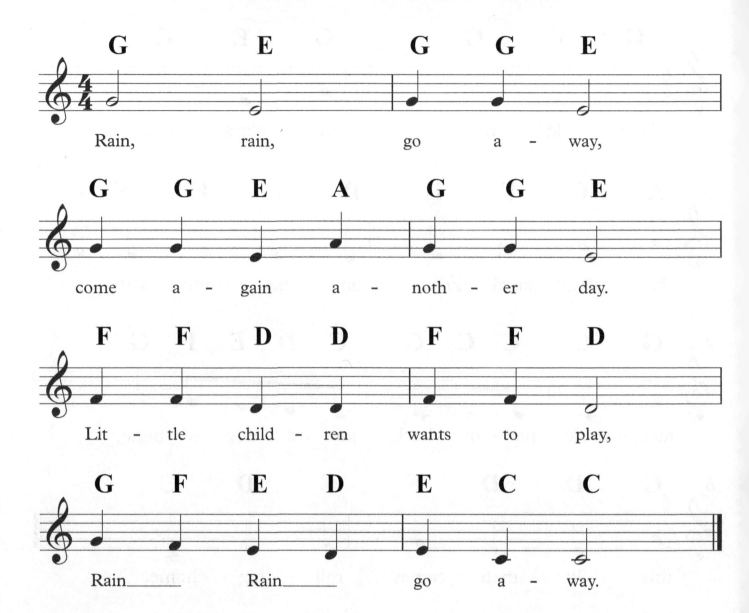

25. Old MacDonald Had A Farm

26. Jingle Bells

68

27. We Wish You A Merry Christmas

We wish you a mer-ry Christ-mas, we wish you a mer-ry

Christ-mas we wish you a mer-ry Christ-mas and a hap-py New

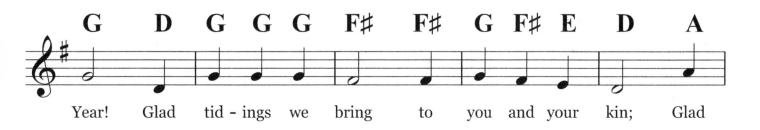

Year! Glad tid-ings we bring to you and your kin; Glad

tid-ings for Christ-mas and a hap-pay New Year! We

wish you a mer-ry Christ-mas, we wish you a mer-ry Christ-mas, we

wish you a mer-ry Christ-mas and a hap-py New Year!

28. Simple Gifts

D D G G A B G B C D D C B A G

'Tis the gift to be sim-ple, 'tis the gift to be free, 'Tis the

A A A G A B A F♯ D D G F♯ G A B A A

gift to come down where we ought to be, And when we find our-selves in the

B C D D A A B A G B A G F♯ G

place just right, 'Twill be in the val - ley of love and de-light.

D B A B C B A G A B B C D C B

When true sim - plic - i - ty is gain'd, to bow and to bend we will

A A B A D G G A B B C D C B

not be a-sham'd, to turn, turn will be our de-light, 'Till by

A A B B A G G G

turn - ing, turn - ing we come 'round right.

29. Oh, Dear! What Can The Matter Be?

Oh, dear! What can the mat-ter be? Oh, dear! What can the mat-ter be?

Oh, dear! What can the mat-ter be? John-ny's so long at the fair.____

He pro-mised to buy me a trin-ket to please me, And

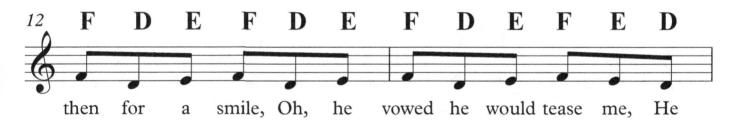

then for a smile, Oh, he vowed he would tease me, He

pro-mised to bring me a bunch of red ro-ses to

tie up my bon-nie brown hair.____

30. O Christmas Tree

31. Hush Little Baby

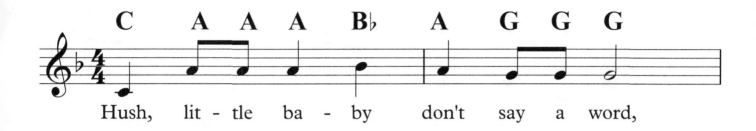

C A A A B♭ A G G G

Hush, lit - tle ba - by don't say a word,

3

C C G G G G A G F F

Pa - pa's gon - na buy you a mock - ing bird.

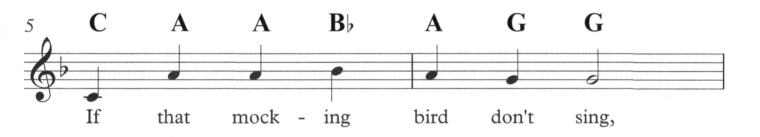

5

C A A B♭ A G G

If that mock - ing bird don't sing,

7

C C G G G G A G F F

Pa - pa's gon - na buy you a dia - mond ring.

32. Away In A Manger

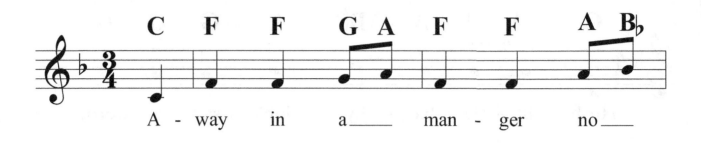

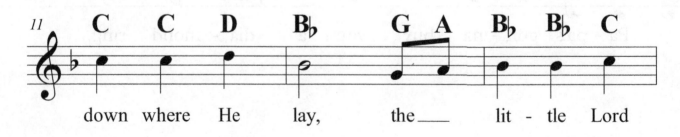

33. Bingo

34. She'll Be Coming Round The Mountain

35. Vacation Days

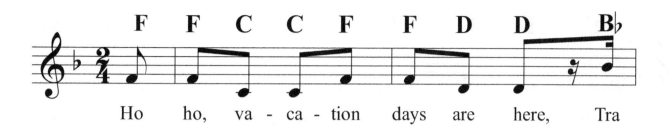

Ho ho, va - ca - tion days are here, Tra

la, tra la, tra la! We wel - come them with

right good cheer, Tra la, tra la, tra la! In

wis - dom's halls we love to be, But yet 'tis plea - sant

to be free. Ho ho, va - ca - tion days are here, Tra

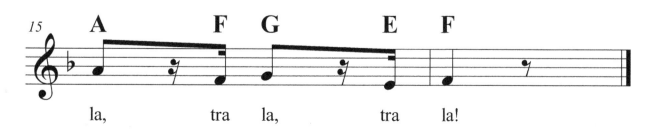

la, tra la, tra la!

36. America

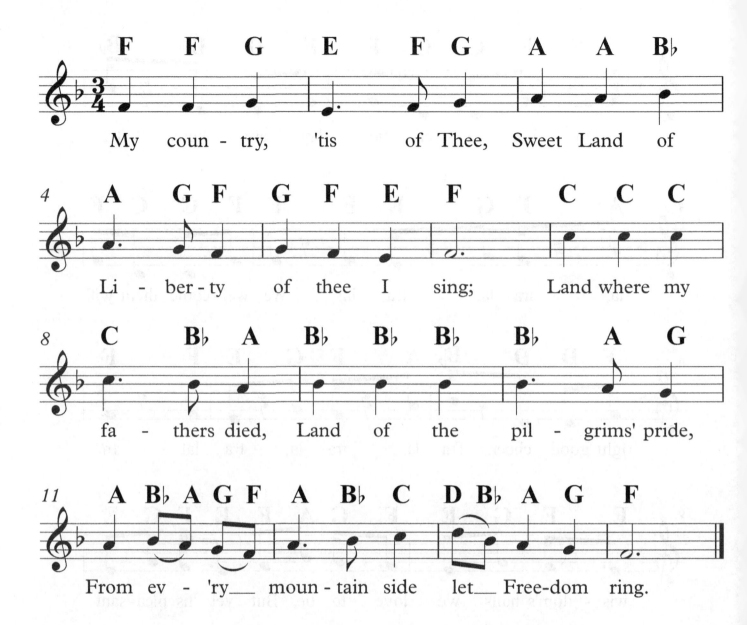

37. Buffalo Gals

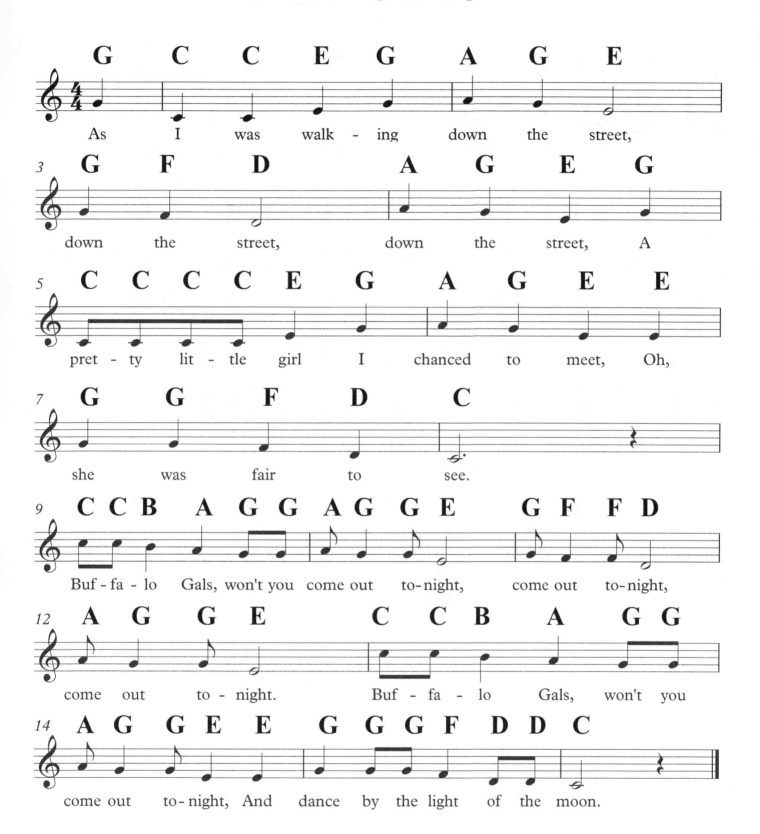

38. Silent Night

39. The North Wind Doth Blow

40. Rock-a-Bye Baby

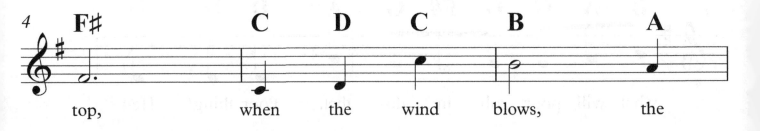

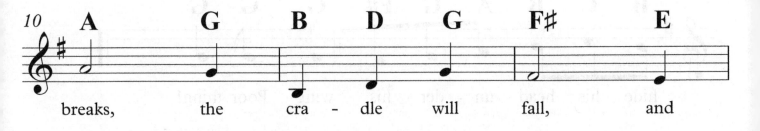

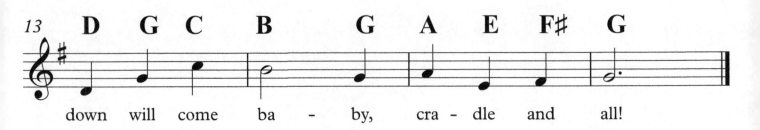

41. Keemo Kymo

42. The Teddy Bears' Picnic

43. I've Got Peace Like A River

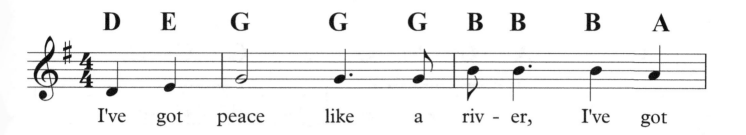

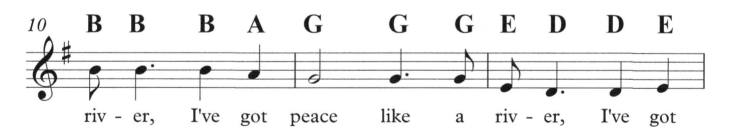

44. Head, Shoulders, Knees and Toes

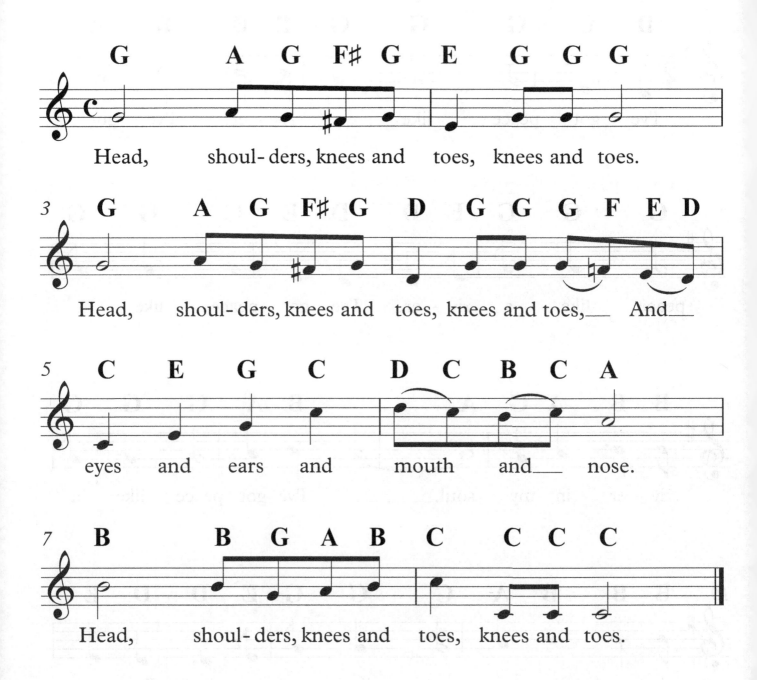

45. Shenandoah

Oh, Shen-nan doah,__ I long to hear you,__ A -

way, you rol - ling ri - ver. Oh,

She - nan- doah,__ I long to hear you,__ A -

way, I'm bound a - way, cross the wide Mis - sou - ri.

46. Clementine

47. Long, Long Ago

48. If You're Happy And You Know It

If you're hap-py and you know it clap your hands. (clap   clap) If you're

hap-py and you know it clap your hands. (clap   clap)   If you're

hap-py and you know it, then your face will sure-ly show it, If you're

hap-py and you know it clap your hands. (clap   clap)

49. All The Pretty Little Horses

Hush - a - bye, don't you cry, go to sleep, my lit - tle

ba - by. When you wake, you shall have

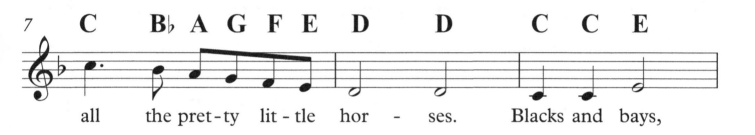

all the pret-ty lit-tle hor - ses. Blacks and bays,

dap-ples and greys, Coach and six a lit-tle hor - ses.

Hush-a-bye, don't you cry, go to sleep my lit-tle ba - by.

50. My Bonnie Lies Over The Ocean

51. Jolly Old Saint Nicholas

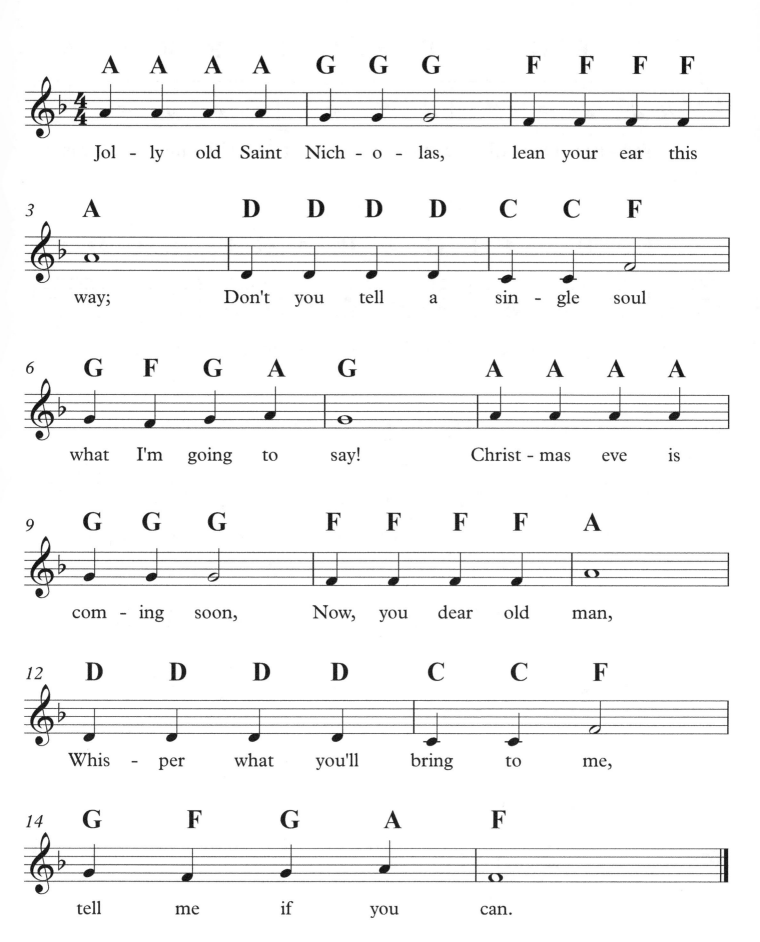

52. Yankee Doodle

53. Cindy

You ought to see my Cin-dy, She lives a-way down

South, And she's so sweet the hon-ey bees, All

swarm a-round her mouth. Get a long home, Cind-dy,

Cin-dy, Get a-long home, Cin-dy, Cin-dy, Get a-long

home, Cin-dy, Cin-dy, I'll mar-ry you some-day.

54. Old Dan Tucker

55. The Cuckoo

56. Aura Lee

As the black-bird in the spring 'neath the wil - low tree, Sat and piped I heard him sing prais - ing Au - ra Lee. Au - ra Lee! Au - ra Lee! Maid of gold - en hair. Sun-shine came a - long with thee and swal - lows in the air.

57. Golden Sun

58. All Through The Night

Sleep, my child and peace at-tend thee All through the

night; Guard - ian an - gels, God will send thee,

All through the night. Soft and drow-sy hours are creep-ing,

Hill and vale in slum-ber sleep-ing, Love a-lone his

watch is keep-ing, All through the night.

59. America The Beautiful

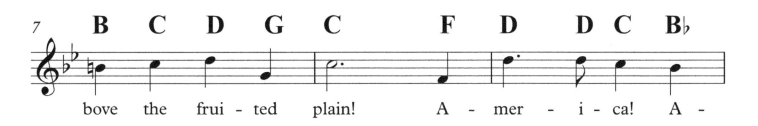

60. Come, All Ye Young Sailormen

E G A G E D D B C D

Come, all ye young sail - or men, lis - ten to

B G F# E F# E D D D

me,___ I'll sing you a song of the

A B A G D B A G

fish of the sea. Then blow, ye winds,

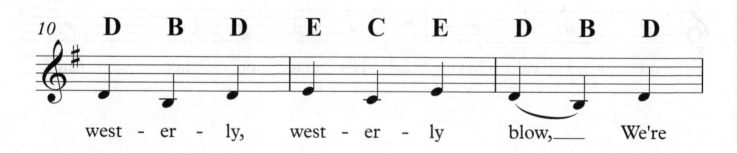

D B D E C E D B D

west - er - ly, west - er - ly blow,___ We're

G A G E D D E G F# G

bound to the south -'ard so stead - y she goes.

Your Bonus *

Link: <u>cutt.ly/DMVusgt</u>

or QR code:

All files are in US Letter format, don't worry if you are using A4 paper, there is almost no difference in these types of paper, so feel free to print on your printer. If the printer asks for the paper size: Specify the paper size that you actually have in the printer.

The folder: **"Files separately"** contains:
1) All songs individually numbered from 1 to 60 together with the song name in the folder: *"All 60 songs Separately"*;
2) Glossary of a Beginner Musician entitled: *"Glossary of a Beginner"*;
3) Letters that can be printed and pasted on the keyboard yourself, file name: *"Letters for the keyboard"*;
4) Keyboard with the designation of each letter on the keys, file name: *"Keyboard with letters"*;
5) All bonus 15 songs separately, folder name: *"Bonus 15 songs separately."*

The folder: **"Main files"** contains:
1) Audio examples of how the song should sound, 75 pieces (60 main + 15 bonus), folder name: *"Audio examples"*;
2) Bonus 15 songs, file name: *"Bonus 15 songs"*;
3) All songs in one file called: *"All 60 songs"*.

* If you have not received a bonus or you have questions, write suggestions here: avgustaudartseva@gmail.com

Thank you for your recent purchase. *We hope you will love it!* If you can, would you consider posting an online review? This will help us continue to provide great products and help potential buyers make confident decisions.

Thank you in advance for your review and for being a preferred customer.

Glossary of a Beginner Musician

 **Stave** (Staff) – five lines and four spaces between them, on which musical notes and other musical signs are written.

 **Notes** – the oval-shaped symbols that are placed on the lines and in the spaces between them.

 Stem – is the part of a note, vertical lines that are directly connected to the note head.

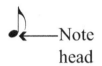 **Note head** – is the part of a note, usually oval. It indicates the pitch (its placement) and duration (its coloring).

 Flag – is the part of a note, whose note value is less than quarter note value.

 **Ledger lines** – short lines which are added to extend the range of the stave when the notes are too low or too high.

 Treble clef – the clef used for notes in the higher pitch ranges.

 **Measure (or Bar)** – the area between two bar lines.

 Bar lines – the lines which cross the stave and divide it into measures (or bars).

Double bar line – is written at the end of a piece of music. It is made up of one thin and one thick line, with the thick line always on the outside.

Note value – the duration of the note.

Whole note – is equal to four counts (or beats).

Whole rest – means the rest for a whole measure; in $\frac{3}{4}$ it receives 3 beats, in $\frac{4}{4}$ it receives 4 beats, in 2/4 it-receives 2 beats.

Half note – is equal to two counts (or beats), two half notes are equal the duration of the one whole note.

Half rest – is equal to half of a whole rest, it is equal to 2 beats.

Quarter note – is equal to one count (or beat), four quarter notes are equal to the duration of one whole note.

Quarter rest – is equal to one quarter of a whole rest, it is equal to 1 beats.

Eighth note – two eighth notes are equal to the duration of one quarter note.

Eighth rest – two eighth rests are equal to the duration of one quarter rest, one eighth rest is equal to half of the value of a quarter rest.

Flat – lowers the pitch.

♯   **Sharp** – raises the pitch.

$\frac{2}{4}$ $\frac{3}{4}$ $\frac{4}{4}$ **Time signature** – appears at the beginning of the music after the clef sign. It contains two numbers, one above the other.

♩.   **Dot after a note** – the note's duration by half the original value.

Octave – the distance between one note and that same note repeated in the next higher or lower register within the audible range.

 **Slur** – smoothly connects two or more notes of different pitches by a curved line over or under the notes.

 **Tie** – joins two notes of the same pitch by a curved line over or under the notes. Each note joined by a tie is held for its full value but only the first note is played or sung.

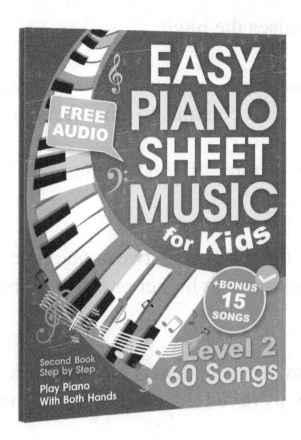

The next step in teaching your child the piano is learning to play with both hands.

The second book smoothly introduces us to the bass clef and how easy it is to learn to play with the left and right hand at the same time. With the help of step-by-step and simple presentation of the material, it will be interesting for your child to continue to explore the amazing and vast world of music!

amazon.com/author/avgusta

A	B	C	D	E	F	G
A	B	C	D	E	F	G
A	B	C	D	E	F	G
A	B	C	D	E	F	G
A	B	C	D	E	F	G
A	B	C	D	E	F	G
A	B	C	D	E	F	G
A	B	C	D	E	F	G
A	B	C	D	E	F	G
A	B	C	D	E	F	G
A	B	C	D	E	F	G
A	B	C	D	E	F	G
A	B	C	D	E	F	G
A	B	C	D	E	F	G

If you do not want to cut from the book - in the folder from page 103 you will find the same files in PDF format and can print at home.

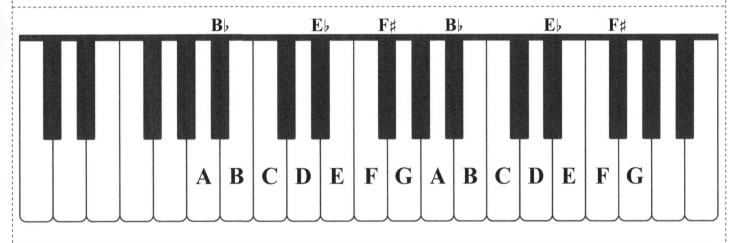

If you do not want to cut from the book - in the folder from page 103 you will find the same files in PDF format and can print at home.

Made in the USA
Middletown, DE
26 August 2024

59813741R00064